Everybody Is a Real-estate Investor
(Yes Even You)

By Andre' Williams Sr.

Copyright © 2018 Andre' Williams Sr.

All rights reserved. No part of this publication may be reproduced, distributed, or transmitted in any form or by any means, including photocopying, recording, or other electronic or mechanical methods, without the prior written permission of the publisher, except in the case of brief quotations embodied in critical reviews and certain other noncommercial uses permitted by copyright law.

For permission requests, write to the author at

andres1995.aw@gmail.com

Ordering Information
For orders visit   www.Amazon.com
www.oneheaveninc.com
Oneheaveninc@gmail.com
Facebook@Oneheaveninc

Cover Illustration Copyright © 2018
By Andre' Williams Sr.
Cover design by Camille Jones
Editing by Joonie Gee
Chapter illustrations by Andre' Williams Sr.
Author photograph by Andre' Williams Sr.

Greetings,

In this book, you will learn a little about the author, you will learn how to flip properties for profit, and you will learn how to pick a great investment team. By the end of this book, you will be able to assess which side of the real-estate investment table you are currently sitting on, decide which side you want to be on, and then take your first steps in that direction.

Preface

Hi. My name is Andre Williams Sr. and I am a Real-estate Investor, Entrepreneur, General Contractor and a Realtor from New Jersey. I am a forty-four-year-old husband and father of five beautiful children.

By the way, being a husband and a father is the best investment I could have ever made. Their love and support, alone, makes me rich in ways money could not buy.

Being the son of the two most incredible parents on the planet has made me the man that I am today.

My mother introduced me to God, and for that I will forever be grateful. I believe her prayers and fasting saved my life when I wasn't even praying for myself. Her constant love for me always brought out the best in me and she always encouraged me to follow my dreams. My mother taught me how to open my heart to all of Gods children.

My works of passion and love for providing safe havens and education for children helped me birth my daycare centers, preschools and my Affordable Housing Program.

Thanks Mom.
Elder Hattie Mae White

My Father is *my guy*; my *best man* who introduced me to the real-estate game and who taught me the construction trade from laying foundations to roofing and everything in between. My dad said, "People will always need a place to live, wherever you go and if you can provide them shelter even in the desert you will never go broke".
Thanks Dad.
Andrew Williams Sr. (Inventor)

Andre Williams, Sr.

"If YOU want things in your life to change, YOU have to change 1ˢᵗ and then YOU can change things in your Life."

2 Corinthians 5:17

Therefore if any man be in Christ, he is a new creature: old things are passed away; behold all things become new.

Table of Contents

Chapters:	Pages
Chapter 1 From Infatuation to Love.	8
Chapter 2. The Investor.	19
Chapter 3. Flipping Houses (Build Your Team	34
Chapter 4. Income Properties.	45
Chapter 5. A Gold Mine in Your Back Yard	52
Chapter 6. Applied Knowledge. Information Is Power.	58
Chapter 7. *HGTV* Is Awesome!	61
Chapter 8. Credit Vs Cash	65
Chapter 9. A Good Man Leaves an Inheritance for His Children's Children	71
Bonus Page **Terms That Only Make Sense in The Real-Estate Industry**	77
Bonus Page II How we used our nonprofit 501C3 to receive property	80
Bonus Page III Naomi Williams Age 9 (Drawing of Dad Profile Page Dedication)	84

"You Are Made In The Image Of God"

YOU WERE CREATED TO OWN REALESTATE

Genesis 1:26-28
And God said, Let us make man in our image, after our likeness: and let them have DOMINION over the fish of the sea, and over the fowl of the air, and over the cattle, and over ALL THE EARTH, and over every creeping thing that creepeth upon the earth

One

From Infatuation to Love

My Early Infatuation

The beginning of my infatuation with real-estate came at an early age for me. I must have been around seven or eight-years-old. I actually grew up thinking that everyone had more than one house, the one they lived in and the other that they used to live in. But then they moved to a bigger house and let someone move in their other, smaller, house and every first of the month you pick up an envelope from your old house with your son and then the two of you would go get his favorite milk shake and catch a drive-in movie together. Lol. Sorry for the run-on. But I gave the pen to my six-year-old self to explain. Point is, boy was I wrong!

Still, my adolescent mind thought, "This is great. I'm going to do this with my children when I get older like dad did with me". I didn't know it at the time, but dad had planted a seed in me that actually groomed me to be the landlord and business owner that I am today. Thanks dad.

Throughout those years, I can remember going to properties with dad and doing work on the weekends. Sometimes I would help with painting or replacing broken windows. One time, I even sat on the roof with my dad and my uncle while they were putting roofing cement tar on the roof. For this reason, I never had a fear of heights. Dad would just say stay away from the edge, etc.

My Teenage Years

I can remember being a teenager in high school. Dad would say, "Hey. Stop by the house on Walnut and pick up the envelope and bring it home with you after school." The high school was right around the corner from this property. One time in particular, a young lady who was a year or two ahead of me in high school, answered the door when I stopped by. She handed me an envelope that was addressed from her parents to my dad. I think the realization started to set in that they were renting our childhood home. I realized that there are different sides of the same table. This is monopoly in real life. I liked being on the side of collecting rent and ownership.

My love for real-estate increased even more because of the game *Monopoly*. I can remember playing this game with my siblings on mom side, my nieces and nephews, my cousins, and my friends. We would play for hours on end. I became so good at it that I invented new ways to keep my opponents in the game even after I had already won. When they'd owe me money and couldn't pay, I would let them stay in the game by taking what they owed for rent from the $200 they collected as they passed *GO*; or I would buy their properties from them to settle their debt. I loved the game. I was a natural! My childhood friends started calling me "Pay Day for Dre" as we played *Monopoly* and other games where accumulating the most money was the reward.

True story. A childhood friend of mine, RIP Dunn, had this awesome PC boxing game that rewarded money purses every time players moved up in the ranks, and of course, he was the best at it. He made the mistake of inviting me in to play. Smh. I quickly caught on to the system and began whooping his butt on his own game. I broke all of his records and Dunney kicked me and the other kids out of his house. Lol. These experiences with my childhood friends planted a seed in me that made me respect money. They also made it come to me more easily. Words are powerful. By my friends speaking the words, "Pay Day for Dre'", I would grow up and attract wealth. By calling me "Pay Day for Dre" and by me winning at *Monopoly* and other currency-based games so easily, the foundation for my future in building wealth was set.

Having had an entrepreneur's heart from a very young age, I ran my paper boy job as if it were my own business. I would pay my little brother to help me some mornings. But, the paper-boy business didn't last long. The manager of our local newspaper tried to cheat me. He hadn't realized that he picked the wrong kid to cheat. But he learned fast after my dad cursed him out and put him out of our house one evening when he came to collect and do breakdown of $$.

Every ending is an opportunity for a new beginning. The end of my paper business opened the doors for a raise in my allowance. I got by on that until I turned fourteen and I got my working papers. Then I got a job at McDonalds. In junior high school by then, I would also work with the Sports Medicine Team. With a solid income, I did the next logical thing. I officially opened up a bank account and I got my first debit ATM card. My first bank was Core State Bank, which has since and through many transitions, become Wells Fargo.

Falling in Love

Fast forward

I was about nineteen or twenty-years-old. The young lady who I was dating at the time knew that I loved Real-estate. So, she bought me a Real-estate Investment Kit complete with workbook and audio cassettes by Carlton Sheets. I can remember listening to the audio books over and over again. What I learned from those audio cassettes became embedded in my soul as well as my psyche. It was all I was interested in listening to when I was driving. Every story captured my imagination and I could visualize myself living through similar scenarios to the ones that the author spoke about. I eventually begin to see other angles not presented by the author. I actually saw myself as the General Contractor and the Investor. Thus began a serious love affair that later blossomed into a marriage.

Thanks BG.

Currently

I now play Monopoly in real life and I teach my children economics this way as well. Since I do not allow my children to watch TV during the week, when we are not at their practices or instrument lessons, we are at Barnes and Nobles buying books or at home playing family games.

We play Monopoly but it's the new improved electronic teller machine version with credit cards for each player. Now, when players pass *GO* instead of collecting $200, they collect $2,000,000.00. And get this, when players land on properties, their payments to the other players is in the millions. This to me is genius especially because I don't want my children growing up being intimidated by numbers. We will talk more numbers in the upcoming chapters. I carefully watch my children as they make decisions to buy properties and negotiate with one another. I see things in them all that allow me to correct or add another perspective, so they could see the big picture. That one day they will inherit my properties and my businesses. I hope that they can take what I've taught them and grow to become owners of shopping plazas, malls, hotels and more. It's all real-estate and very profitable. I spend time with my children this way because they all have gifts. As parents we want to help nurture those gifts. I can see them put two and two together when I take them with me to collect rent or visit our daycares and preschools and I make references to these businesses during our Monopoly games. We even talk about banking as we make real deposits, we have conversations about credit and maintaining a clear level head to make good business decisions. So, no matter which way my children decide to go in life in pursuit of their own dreams and goals, real-estate ownership is a must. Not only because I will leave them an inheritance which will include properties, but because of the fundamentals that I am teaching them now. They just may take it to another level and exceed my dreams. Nonetheless,

Everybody is A Real-estate Investor and I'm preparing my children to continue sitting on the owner's side of the table. I suggest you so the same.

Most people say "they are afraid to own a home". Nothing to fear, you are investing already.

"Fear stands for False, Evidence, Appearing, Real"

2 Timothy 1:7

For God has not given us a spirit of fear, but of power and of love and of a sound mind

Two

The Investor

There are several types of investors in real-estate. This chapter will discuss five types; the renter, the landlord, the homeowner, the wholesaler, and the tax lien investor.

First, let's look at the renter and the landlord. I look at these investment opportunities from many different perspectives, and one can't prosper without the other; so whether you are paying rent to someone or collecting rent from someone, both parties have an agreement to *invest* in the property.

The Renter/Lessee

Let's take a look at this type of Investor.

The renter pays rent to a landlord through an agreement called a lease or a rental agreement for the benefit of residing in a property that is owned by the landlord. Some rental agreements are still done by the good old hand shake if the parties involved have a good rapport. I prefer written rental agreements. Be it family or friends, people tend to change; especially when money is involved, so it's best to protect yourself as the owner with a written agreement. That's the only thing the courts will consider if it came down to it.

As the renter occupies the dwelling, the renter must manage his or her rented home's day to day up-keep. However, as the landlord is the owner of the property, when major maintenance or repair is needed, such as a repair to a leaking roof or to a broken furnace, the landlord will pick up that expense unless otherwise agreed upon. Let's say, for instance, something breaks in the home such as the stove, refrigerator, or hot water heater. It is best that renting contracts clearly stipulate what would be handled and by whom.

The rental contracts can be drawn up by the two individuals or by an attorney. Sample rental and sales agreements can be found online. Real-estate kits that include all types of fill in the blank real-estate contracts and agreements can be found in any local office supply store. They do come in handy.

Now that we know a bit more about the rental contract and about some rental obligations, let's look more closely at the investment aspect of being a renter.

Let's do some math for the renter .

Property A rents for $900 per month. You (the renter)

have a one-year rental agreement.

Calculate: $900 monthly rent X 12 months = $10,800 yearly investment.

So, in one year, you invest $10,800 into the property. Now consider your investment over multiple years; say, 2, 3 or 4 years. Let's review your investment.

Calculate $900 monthly rent X 24 months = $21,600 total investment.

Calculate $900 monthly rent X 36 months = $32,400 total investment.

Calculate $900 monthly rent X 48 months = $43,200 total investment.

The renter, over four years has invested $43,200 which is a great investment. It pays for a roof over your head, some peace of mind when it comes to major repairs, and less responsibility.

The renter enjoyed providing a home for themselves and family and created many wonderful memories in the process. At the end of rental agreement, the only asset gained by the renter is the return of the security deposit provided that the rental property was left in acceptable condition. Some land lords allow their tenants to do sweat equity in the beginning of a lease contract in place of a down payment. Some allow this practice at the end of a lease contract for the return of the security deposit. The catch is you must give the property back to the land Lord the way they gave it to you or deductions from security deposit can incur costs. In my twenty years of being a landlord, no one ever gave me a property back in the same condition I gave it to them.

Other than the security deposit, all of the rent paid helped to build equity for the property owner and that stays with the property and owner. That's the difference between assets and Liabilities.

Owning homes, as opposed to renting them, creates actual assets for the owner. Renting homes is more or less a liability in the end. In the end, considering what you have learned here, hopefully you will be encouraged to grab a seat on the other side of the table; at least to become a homeowner.

The Landlord

Let's take a look at this type of Investor.

One may become a landlord by a number of means. Some landlords inherit properties. Some landlords purchase properties with cash and some purchase through mortgages with banks and other creative lending sources. None the less, the landlord is the property owner; the title and deed holder of property.

The landlord has the awesome job of collecting rent and taking care of the major problems with property that he is leasing out unless otherwise specified in the rental agreement.

Now, let's look at some numbers to see what this side of the investment table looks like.

Property B: The current Rent is $1500 per month. The landlord has leased his property for the past three years.

Calculate $1500 monthly rent received X 36 months = $54,000 yearly income from just one investment rental property. Not a bad income for three years. Now, imagine that this landlord investor has more than one property; say three with similar numbers.

Calculate $1500 monthly rent received X 36 months X

three properties = $162,000 total income from these investment rental properties. We can agree that this landlord investor is doing more than okay financially.

The landlord investor has obligations, though. We have touched upon the obligation to maintain the major aspects of the property. There are also financial obligations such as, repair and maintenance costs, property taxes, and property insurance. These are part of the landlord's financial investment, in other words, what the landlord pays into the property.

The landlord may also invest money in a property to reside in. Though many homeowners may also choose not to be landlords. There are pros and cons to sitting on both sides of this table as well.

Like with *Monopoly*, I chose to own properties and sit on this side of the table for the long haul. I also enjoy flipping properties. We will speak about that in the upcoming chapters. For now, let's talk about the third investor type; the homeowner.

The Homeowner

Homeowners, believe it or not, are investors too; ones whose attention is focused on the property in which they reside. Because they typically take pride in their homes, homeowners keep their homes beautiful inside and out. They become invested in their neighborhoods as their interest is in safety and the value of their property. To this end, they develop neighborhood watch programs and they look out for one another.

I enjoy talking to homeowners and I always make sure to give them my number in the neighborhoods where I have investment properties. Although I do not reside in my investment properties, I share a goal of keeping the neighborhoods safe and property values at their maximum.

Of course, in my own neighborhood, I often commune with my neighbors. We help one another throughout the year from help with shoveling snow and raking leaves to keeping watch over one another's property while on vacation. Homeowners experience a unique type of pride in their own homes. Everyone should have this experience.

FLIPPING REAL-ESTATE

Flipping real-estate is fun, exciting, and can be very lucrative. Properties such as, HUD properties, foreclosures, or bank owned properties can be purchased below market value. It is best to aim for 40% to 70 % below market value in order to make a decent profit. Educate yourself on the current market values and remain within that range. Otherwise, you can get creative with your design style and colors.

Normally my team secure suburban properties where current market values range from 150k to 250k. We buy a property for less than 70k and we invest around 30k in repairs. When complete, we sell for a minimum of 150k. That is a profit of $50k, which is great for a couple months' worth of work. This investment type is all about building the right team. A good realtor, general contractor, architect, title company, attorney and lender is the making of a good investor.

Wholesale Real-estate Investor

I had my first experience at whole selling properties over ten years ago when it wasn't as popular a term as it is today. We just helped other investors get great deals on properties. We didn't want or have the man power to do as many deals. We did contracts and bought for a lower price then found another investor and sold to them at a slightly higher price most times the same day.

I actually became involved with wholesaling by accident.

My buddy called me while the family and I were on vacation in sunny Orlando, Florida. I can remember as clear as day. We were all in the minivan heading back to our resort when my phone rang. I wasn't going to answer. But, since my buddy didn't call very often, something just told me to answer.

"Hello." He said. "Dre' I want to invest in real-estate and I have no clue how to get started."

So I told him one of the ways I buy properties was by

riding through urban neighborhoods like where we grew up in Trenton, NJ. When I'd come across boarded up properties, I would note the addresses. Once I had about ten or so properties' address, I'd call the local property tax collectors' office at city hall. I'd find out what is owed in back taxes. And If the amount due is under 10k, I'd find out the name and address of the party or parties responsible for those taxes. Once a list is secured, I'd write letters to the owners of those properties. In the letter we would introduce ourselves as cash buyers and offer to make an offer on the property. We would be sure to advise the owner that we have done due diligence and that we are aware of the amount owed in back property taxes. Sometimes we'd hit gold. Other times we'd miss. But when we hit, we normally hit a pretty good deal. One time in particular we hit a property tax lien investor who had liens on lots of properties. The investor only wanted to make 18% interest on the tax liens and wasn't really interested in the properties. We became a good source for them to unload the foreclosed properties they accumulated over time. They would send us a list of properties and cut us a deal on ten to fifteen properties at a time. We would sell some properties to other investors at a figure a little higher than what we purchase them for. This is what is considered Whole Selling today.

There are individuals now who wholesale properties for a living. They have created a network of cash buyers, they build a network of leads to get HUD properties, bank owned properties, and more before they hit the hard real-estate market. Some even link their investors to hard money lenders and a list of contractors.

These wholesalers put the scope of work together for investors and paint the entire picture so that the investor sees the purchase price rehab cost and resale price and estimated profit margin. They make 5k to 10k per deal they close. They don't have to get involved with the construction rehab phase. They make their wholesale profit upfront at the closing.

Now that we have an understanding of the types of investors there are, and we have decided which side of the investment table we wish to be on, let's explore how to get started.

"I will give you houses you didn't build and vineyards you didn't plant"

Joshua 24:13

So I gave you a land on which you not toil and cities you did not build; and you live in them and eat from vineyard and olive groves that you did not plant;

Three

Flipping Real Estate
(Build Your Team)

For investors wanting to sit on this side of the table, you'll want to build a team to help meet your goals for *Returns On Investments.*

1. A good Realtor or Broker is essential. Your agent will help you identify properties like fixer uppers to buy and your agent will help you find a buyer to purchase your property once completed. There is nothing like having a good Real-estate Agent on your team.

2. Secure the services of a lender. A lender could be a mortgage company, private lender, credit union, a group of hard money investors, or a regular bank. A lender could even be a group of friends and family

members that you pay back with interest over time.

3. General Contractor: This is the person responsible for the construction and usually the GC will help procure your subcontractors, Plumbers, Electricians, HVAC etc.

4. Title Company or Real-estate Attorney: The purpose of the title company is to make sure that you receive a property free and clear of any liens or mortgages and with title insurance. This protects you as a buyer and later on as a seller. All types of liens can be placed on a property and the title company usually goes back fifty years to make sure no previous owner had outstanding liens on the property.

For example, early in my investment days I had a seller sell a property to us and instead of traditional, real-estate sales agreement, we transferred ownership through Quit Claim Deed, meaning a short form and quick way to transfer the property over to my company and when I got the title work done, they found out that the owner who owned the home before the previous owner had had an exterior siding job done on the property. The construction company placed a $5k lien on the property for payment of the siding job. Though this occurred about twenty years prior to my ownership of the property, I had to have the lien removed in order to move forward with my goals for the property. So, my title company had to track down the owner in question; a woman in Brooklyn, New York.

Since we were familiar with the woman, the previous owner and myself were able to travel to her home where she was able to provide us with evidence that she had satisfied the contract between herself and the construction company. We were able to have the construction lien removed from the property. If I had not done this, we would have had to send this company a check for $5k dollars at the closing table which would have dug into my profit. Having a good title company, for me, meant the difference between a $40 trip to Brooklyn and a $5,000 payment. That's how important title companies are.

Working together with these people from these four facets of real-estate make life a lot easier when flipping properties.

I, personally, enjoyed this side of investing so much that I ended up getting my real-estate license. I enjoyed doing the work on the properties ever since my dad had taught me the trades. So, I ended up getting my General Contractor License as well. When I first started out, I got money and loans from friends and family to purchase the properties I wanted to flip. I paid them back with interest once I sold the properties.

Now, it is possible to just hire these individuals. But, I was just crazy enough to invest in myself to do it all. I wanted to be in control of my own time line. I use to believe that the only person I would bet on was me. I had a sickening work ethic when I started buying properties. I'm more balanced now, though, since I have kids and a family. I have come to appreciate the value in a strong team.

Once you have your team, you are ready to begin flipping. The whole idea is to buy the property, rehabilitate it, and then to sell it for at least two to three times what you paid for the property. There are so many creative ways to buy fixer uppers or flipping properties. We purchase some through foreclosures. We purchase some abandoned properties, some distressed properties, and some short sales. Some properties we acquire through donations, sheriff sales, or auctions. We would even purchase ten to fifteen properties at a time as I touched on in the wholesale section.

We would contact our tax lien investor and say what do you got for us. The older gentlemen would say. I will fax you over a list of what I have now and what we are foreclosing on and you Pick what you want and I will cut you a great deal.
He gave us a price of 3k per house on fifteen houses so the total would come to $45k.

We would sell seven houses at 7k per house which would be $49k. We paid 45k for all fifteen properties. We sold seven properties and kept eight properties for our own inventory to rehabilitate. Which means we ended up with eight free houses and a profit of 5k after wholesaling seven properties to other investors.

We sold seven properties. The seven that we sold to another investor paid for the entire fifteen; so we ended up with eight free properties in this deal from a gentleman that bought tax liens, they foreclosed on the tax liens and then ended up with the properties after a certain length of time.

It was the wholesaling that intrigued me the most. It was Tax Lien Investment that accrued 18% interest daily.

TAX LIEN INVESTOR

Purchasing tax liens is a business within itself because in most tax sales an 18% interests is attached to the lien and it accrues at 18% every single day until it's paid.

For example: Let say the tax lien was $1.00 by

Compound Interests! $3.17 in less 8 Days a 200% Profit	Day 2	$1.18
	Day 3	$1.39
	Day 4	$1.64
	Day 5	$1.94
	Day 6	$2.28
	Day 7	$2.69

So in less than seven days you will more than double your money in buying tax liens. Check with your local property tax collectors' office for tax sales rules and guidelines at your local city hall. Interest rates may differ and the length of time before you can foreclose on the tax sale certificate may vary to from state to state. Most investors that buy the tax liens rarely want the properties, they are really after that amazing 18% interest daily accruals. I tried to go back and buy a home that I could have bought when I was nineteen but passed on it for sentimental reasons I later bought tax liens on that property, hoping that I could foreclose on it and retrieve the property but later that year I got a huge check in the mail for like thirty times what I paid for the tax lien. Bitter sweet, the money was great to have but I really wanted the property instead. You win some and you change your perception of the loss and it becomes a lesson so you still win at the end of the day.

Consider the tax lien industry as a complete business. You have individuals that go to the tax liens sales with 5k and rack up on just buying tax lien.

People Like To Say

"Where ever you Go, there you are"
 but I like to say.
"Where ever you Go, God can meet you there!"

Deuteronomy 31:6
Be Strong and courageous. Do not be afraid or terrified because of them, for the lord your God goes with you and he will never leave you or abandon you

Four

Income Properties

Remember. My dad told me and I told you that no matter where you go people will always need a place to live. Another saying in real-estate, even to this day, is "they are not making any more land, so whatever is out there, buy it because God isn't adding on more land to what we have now".

This brings us to the real oldest profession in the world, income properties. In the beginning, we traded agriculture, animals, and seeds. But whoever controlled the land, probably had the most animals and agriculture because they could afford to feed them and cultivate it. Not to mention, those who didn't own the land paid the landowners to use the land. There is wealth in ownership.

We often think that when we retire our pensions will be enough to help us maintain a good lifestyle, but too often we see people struggle more after retirement. In some cases, they even have to pick up a part time job at 60 and 70 years old. Retirement is a time in one's life when people should be living it up. Becoming a real-estate investor can make this dream a reality. There are, for example, duplexes and multifamily properties that can yield a very nice income allowing investors to retire comfortably.

This next paragraph is a little personal but befitting of the topic of income properties. I knew an older woman who owned four properties, one right next to the other. Two of the properties where single family semi-detached homes. The other two properties had three apartments in each. I later learned that after my mom and dad divorced, my dad kept buying houses and my mom became a renter. My mother rented one of the older woman's houses for about nineteen years along with her new husband. He wasn't taught to be a homeowner unlike my dad. So, one day, I decided to calculate the rent that my mother had paid to this woman over the course of nineteen years. It blew my mind! My mother paid $700 per month for nineteen years; that is $159,600. My mother paid for this house about three times in the time that she rented it.

Had she bought it instead renting in the 80s I'm sure she could have bought it for $30k to $40k. The property value increased over time almost doubling in the almost twenty years of renting. She also helped pay for the older woman car payments, deposits towards her kids' college and maybe even paid down the mortgage on the older woman's own house. Long story short, as my mother grew older, I told mom that enough was enough; and quite frankly, it is every little boy's dream to buy his mom a house. By that time, I was in my thirties; and even though my mom was married, I felt it was my responsibility to do it. So, I did. The opportunity came when the new house she was renting went into foreclosure and the realtor that the bank hired stopped by to begin having my mom forward the rent to them instead of to the previous owner. I told my mom to tell the realtor that I was interested in buying the house cash and could close in a couple of weeks. He said the house is worth $250k but the bank only wants $45k. Needless to say, SOLD! I bought the house for my mom, built her a full bathroom on the first floor in her bedroom to make it convenient for her, and all she has to pay now is $1500 a year in property taxes and $600 a year in property insurance. The House has eight bedrooms and three bathrooms. My mother rents rooms out to her care takers and other family members. She had joined me in becoming a real-estate investor. We turned my mother's rented home into an income property for her. How awesome is that? Love Mom.

Here is an actual income property that we purchased rehabilitated and now are in the process of holding the mortgage note for 1 of my tenants through our Affordable Housing Program.

.

Paid 7k Worth $80k
It cost us About $25k To Resurrect this One. It Actually had no floors and everything from the roof on down collapsed into the basement. We could not walk into this house when we first purchased it. We had to stick a ladder down into basement on rubble for me and the guys to clean it out. The only thing saved this house from completing collapsing was it was brick and a row home. This property was exciting to put back together. We nick named it Iraq. It has all new plumbing, electrical, framing etc.

This property use to be a 2 bedroom 1 Bathroom but we had our Architect draw it up for a 3 Bedroom 2 Full Bathrooms

When we showed up the neighbors said knock down that old ugly house. They didn't see the potential. Once it was done, they all wanted to buy it. That's how God see us when people don't see our true value. God do!

"ONE HEAVEN INC. SLOGAN IS RESURRECTING FAMILIES, HOMES AND DREAMS"

"This is Why"

Five

A Gold Mine in Your Back Yard

Most urban and suburban areas around the globe have hidden gold mines for investors. The city of Philadelphia has over 20,000 abandoned properties that are losing property tax revenue every year. Cities like this are looking for creative investors to come in and to help get these properties back on the tax books. Most of the time, when this type of tax revenue is lost, public libraries, public recreational pools and public gyms are closed down. After school programs are shut down and city jobs are lost. Basic maintenance is neglected, and the streets have pot holes everywhere. When these cities lose revenue from taxes, the county budget is affected and sometimes even the state budget is affected. Hard working people who are potential owners who would take pride in the neighborhoods begin to move away.

As a result, the areas transform into crime infested and drug infested neighborhoods.

Investors have a keen eye for the potential in such areas. When people are leaving these neighborhoods, we take it as a sign for us to come and invest. We know that the potential is there for us to buy low and rehabilitate; thereby, increasing the value and attracting owners back into these neighborhoods. Owners who will become part of the gentrification and bring revenue back to the areas allowing for renewal of programs and improvement of the quality of life of those who live in the improved areas. I've seen the value of brown stones in areas that were once abandoned, skyrocket into the hundreds of thousands; even millions once they had been updated.

Contractors Do's

When choosing your team be sure to get bids from at least three general contractors who are licensed and insured to do work in your area. A lot of the rehab work will require permits; so you want to choose a company that knows the rules, codes, and regulations for their trade. Always do written agreements with your contractors and sub-contractors. Never give any tradesmen all of the money up front. Do at least two to three draw payments based on stages of work completed. This will eliminate contractors wasting time and your money. Set deadlines and realistic goals. Make sure all of your subcontractors, electricians, plumbers and HVAC technicians are licensed and insured; this for safety reasons as well. You don't want any mistakes being made or any workers or people getting hurt as a result of work performed on your properties. Safety first.

Choosing materials appliances and paints should be

done by you, the investor, to ensure that its quality is to your liking. I have to remember that I approach things from a different angle than most people because I'm the investor and I'm also the GC; but I advise other investors who have to deal with GCs to get involved with buying materials and learning prices of materials like sheetrock, windows, light fixtures, sink and tub fixtures, flooring, and more. Learn how to pick through different brands of paints. Set up accounts with your local home improvement and paint stores; as well as lumber supply stores so that you can get the same discounts that contractors get.

It's an exhilarating feeling when you are working on your first property and you see it begin to come together. Before you know it, you are leaving the closing table with a check. We have a saying, CTC, meaning "cut the check". **Lol. Don't be afraid to get your hands a little dirty and learn as much as you can about the industry that you are investing i1 way or another.**

"Without A Vision, The People Will Perish"

Habakkuk 2:2

Write the vision and make it plain so that those that read it can run with it.

This Property is an actual before and after picture of 1 of the boarded properties that we rehabilitated in Trenton NJ. We paid 5k for it and when the market was up it was worth $135,000. We invested about $25k into the property to rehab.
Not a bad profit margin.

Six

Applied Knowledge Is Power

There are so many real-estate investment opportunities all around us if we pay attention to them. From residential, commercial to building brand new. I took the knowledge and skills training that my dad provided to me and the passion and creativity I learned while playing *Monopoly* and gaining my real-estate license and general contracting license, and I have made a career and birthed businesses and opened schools out of this knowledge. The he, my dad, learned as a young man and taught to me.

Before I hire guys in my construction company now, we train them first. Eventually they will attend our Private Career School Fresh Start Training Academy, LLC. before we offer them a job. We want to equip them with the necessary knowledge and training to keep up with the demands of our business. We want to ensure that the new trainees are as knowledgeable as our more seasoned employees who have been working with us some close to two decades. We want to also implement training employees in several areas that we want to invest in in the near future as we convert some houses into assisted living complexes. We are looking to invest in franchises, hotels, shopping malls, and more.

"The richest place on earth is the grave yard. So many unfulfilled dreams died with the people that didn't believe enough to manifest them. So many unwritten songs, inventions, manuscripts, movies and more. I urge you to dig up those old dreams and work on them, even if you got to touch it a little bit every day. That's progress."

Seven

HGTV is Awesome!

The shows that come on television about rehabilitating properties has made a lot of people interested in investing in real-estate. That is great. Just keep in mind that what they show you in a thirty-minute TV show, but in reality, it actually took weeks or months to complete.

Here's a bit more about my first experiences with flipping homes. This should give you a sense of how involved the process is.

Like I mentioned before, I made an $80k profit on my first flip. The property that I flipped next was on the market for $13k. I originally viewed the property as a realtor. Still, I was a licensed GC as well. So I advised the sellers not to renew the listing agreement if the property did not sell within the contracted time of the listing agreement. I told them to contact me instead.

When the property didn't sell, the owner contacted me and I made them an offer that put the owners in the position to invest. I offered them $24k for the property. But there would be a small condition. The owners would have to deed the property over to me while I rehabilitated it. I planned to make it into a two-family home and I would do the entire job myself. Under the terms of our agreement, I would pay them the $24k when the job was done and once I sold the property. Anything over the $24k would be my profit since I'd taken all of the risk and incurred all of the expenses.

We sold the house for $125k after it was rehabbed. We netted close to 90k profit. Furthermore, each apartment in the newly rehabbed property generated about $1600 a month for the new investor that bought the property. That was the difference the knowledge of the industry made hence the licenses taught me how to spot deals, how to negotiate and then do the rehab with my construction company.

Anything can be fixed with the right tools, so it is doable with the right team. I always encourage people to make sure you partner up with a GC if nothing else. With the expertise they bring to the table, the GC is the most important ally when it comes to fixer uppers. Though it will not be done in thirty-minutes as seen on TV, having the right team will help you get the job done.

"Don't let anyone tell you that buying houses with no money down or having someone give 1 to you for free is IMPOSSIBLE. The word itself says I'M POSSIBLE"

And I'm Living Proof in Faith

Hebrews 11:6 Without Faith it is impossible to please God, because anyone who comes to him must believe that he exists and that he rewards those who earnestly seek him.

Eight

Credit Vs Cash

I come from a cash background and was taught back when I was growing up in the 90s that if you didn't have the cash to buy it, you don't need it. By thinking this way, it forced me to be creative with purchasing properties and finding money to rehab them. It also allowed me to buy properties for cash which meant that I would own them free and clear of any mortgages.

I looked at the income tax season as a great time to teach friends and family members how to invest their cash for a good profit. This worked well for me when I first started flipping properties. Now that the properties are coming so fast, I had to start listening to credit builders and credit unions to learn how to use other people's money to help us close on deals faster and finish bigger projects quicker as well.

I recommend you, to obtain your credit report and see what your score is and if it's below 580, get help. One of the easiest ways to start building your credit is to get a department store credit card. You can also apply for online credit cards retail stores; even gas cards are fairly easy to get, and the idea is to keep a high available credit balance. Try not to use more than 10% of your credit card available balance. Pay off what you do use quickly, and your scores will increase dramatically. We call it the 10% utilization rule. Some say 30% but to get the best results don't use more than 10%. If you have creditors that you owe, you can call them and negotiate a lower payment option. The key is communication. We apply for hotel credit cards and get award points even airline credit cards that partner with banks. This will allow you to not only build up your credit but rewards that will put you in a position to travel for discounts or even free. The banks like to give money and credit to people that don't look like they need It. Totally opposite of what we thought. But they figure if you have great scores and high available balances it looks like you manage your money and credit very well. You can build and restore your credit on your own. For those who want to hire companies to do it, there are plenty of credit repair companies out there.

Here is a company that I used when I wanted to build my personal and business credit www.fundandgrow.com . For credit restoration you can go to www.LexingtonLaw.com website. The scoring cycle is like every thirty days. I used a free app at www.creditkarma.com to keep track of my scores once I got serious about building credit. I told my team that we all need to hit at least 800 credit scores. For some, it was easy for others it's a reachable goal and a work in progress. Now that you are a part of our team. We need you in the 800s.

If you got your scores up into the high 600's and 700's or 800's, you can practically get anything you want regarding loans and credit cards and credit lines to grow your real-estate investment business. Unfortunately, they didn't teach us anything about credit when we were in high school or college and by the time we got our first credit card in our early twenties we weren't knowledgeable enough to maintain them responsibly. That's surely not the way that I am raising my children now.

Business credit puts you on a whole other level that personal credit can't provide. You can actually achieve higher credit limits especially if your business has a good income source.

Personal credit scores coupled with assets that are owned free and clear can also be borrowed against to help you increase a better return on investments.

"In the Last 4 years of my life I began to feed my spirit more that I do my flesh. Each level that we go to in life the more discipline we must become, and knowledgeable about how to protect what you have gained. A good parent must prepare their children for their passing. We must begin having conversations about leaving Wills. Especially if you are jumping into the real estate game on this side of the table."

Nine

A Good Man Leaves an Inheritance to His Children's Children

"A Good Man Leaves An Inheritance To His Children's Children and the Wealth of The Wicked Is Laid Up For The Just" Proverbs 13:22

When I read this old proverb it makes perfect sense to me because I am living proof that the knowledge that parents have learned and then have taught me has put me in a position to provide for myself and my children. Now, I am putting plans in place to leave my unborn grandchildren an inheritance, spiritually and financially.

Imagine if each person was taught this concept. This

powerful concept will allow families to teach their children the importance of maintaining good credit and of the value in becoming owners and investors so that they are prepared once we they reach the age of eighteen. If every person who has children build enough wealth in their own life time to ensure that, at least, two generations of their children attain an inheritance and passed along this concept to each generation, we could tackle some serious issues that plague humanity such as hunger and poverty. And I think the world would be a much better place and that we would have a lot less selfish people.

I personally don't let my children watch television, play video games or play on computers phones or electronics during the week because I want to weed out the distractions and noise that social media and television programming can inflict on our youth. I want to be the one programming my children's minds by imparting things that will boost their creativity and stimulate their growth. So they play instruments, read several books a month a piece and everything that they touch or read they maintain the information and excel in their studies.

During Parent Teacher Conferences their teachers use to ask why our children are so bright and excel in everything they do. It's because they don't have all the clutter to sort through like the other children and adults. It teaches them discipline and focus and to achieve anything great in life, there has to be a great sacrifice. I want them to achieve everything that they are purposed to do in life.

There is an abundance of knowledge available to us, but people can truly only do what they are taught. Once we obtain these jewels, we must leave a blue print for the next generation to follow in our own families. This is how generational blessings are passed down. We can leave financial inheritances to our children by encouraging individuals to write wills and teaching individuals to maintain insurance policies with clear instructions in their wills on how they'd wish to have their assets distributed. This affective system will allow more children to go to college or start businesses and to purchase property.

We also have to begin teaching the younger generation how to manage and maintain the properties especially if it's left as an inheritance. They need to understand how to recognize and appreciate the value of their assets. Remember that everybody will need a place to live, no matter where you live on the planet. So, whether your goal is to purchase rental properties or just a home to live in, pull a team together and apply the collective knowledge that all of you bring to the table. With this information you can pull together an investment group of friends or family members and do business together. Break generational curses by doing something in your family that has never been done. There's enough to go around.

We all have the same potential and the same 24 hours in a day. How will we spend it? Do you want more? Then write out your vision. Chart it out on paper or on a poster or in your planner. We call them vision boards or blue prints.

A vision board or blueprint for your life and goals will allow you to complete your vision by following what you originally set out to do. I encourage everyone to quiet their inner mind and allow yourself to hear from the creator. You are meant to do great things.

Live a full life and empty out all of your dreams so that when your evening comes to an end you can rest assured that you have invested your talents and that you have become a profitable servant to God and to your family. Leave your mark on the world.

Blessings to you!

"The Real estate industry has made more millionaires than any other industry hands down. It's the oldest profession and it's fast pace as well. We often use terms that will only make sense if you are in this industry buying and selling etc. We have included a couple bonus pages."

Bonus I:
Terms That Only Make Sense in The Real-Estate Industry

Renter = individuals who pay rent in exchange for residence.

Landlord = the owner of an investment property. Residential or commercial.

Tenant = a person or company that rents or lease a property.

Homeowner = a person who owns a home.

Sweat Equity = man hours invested in maintaining property.

Leasing = another word for renting

Property Management = A person or company that would be the middle man or manager of a property.

Real-estate Agent = a licensed individual in the area of real-estate guidelines in a specific state. They usually help you buy or sell real-estate and have a fiduciary relationship with their client.

Broker = a licensed and insured individual that's overseeing the real-estate office. The agent works under a licensed broker.

Quit Claim Deed = a short form way to transfer ownership of a property

Rental Agreement = a contract between landlord and tenant specifying terms.

Return On Investment = this refers to the profit an investor makes over top of money initially invested. So if invest $1.00 with you and you gave me .50 extra. My ROI would 50%.

Equity = this refers to the difference between what was paid for a property and what it is actually worth.

For example, I paid $1.00 for the property but it was worth $5.00. Then my equity would be $4.00. The difference between what is paid and what it's worth.

"You Are Blessed To Be A Blessing"

Share what you have learned. I AM!

Bonus II: How We Get Properties Donated to our Nonprofit 501c3.

I watched a particular building for about two years staking it out to be home for our daycare and preschools.

This huge building was boarded up, but It was perfect for our school as it had classrooms, a basketball gymnasium, an auditorium that I thoughts would be perfect for graduations, recitals; the whole nine. It also had a full commercial kitchen in the basement. It was awesome. So, I said maybe I can get it for the back taxes, foreclose on it after two years and it would be ours. I called the tax collector for a year and a half straight and each quarter the taxes were current. Something told me to call my attorney and I asked him how is it that this property is boarded up and for two years straight, yet taxes have been current.

He said, "Hold on. Give me the address and I will look it up." I heard him chuckle. He said, "Look up the street. Do you see a church and a personage?"
I said, "Yeah I do."

He said, "That building the other two properties are owned by the Catholic church. They are tax exempt like your 501c3."

A light bulb went off as soon as he said that. I wasn't disappointed but more or less open to the new world of opportunities that opened up to me. He had no clue but I knew that it was never about me getting that location but the information I would gain from it would help other nonprofit and 501c3s that wanted to help revitalize their communities.

The Catholic Church has set an amazing blue print that provides housing, education, medical care, insurance, jobs, and so much more to families in communities all over the world. If we, as nonprofits, can do just a small part in the communities we are pillars in, we can really empower people.

This Page is dedicated to my daughter Naomi 9 Years old at the time she drew this profile pic of me. I promised her that the drawing would be in my 1st book. So, this makes her a published artist at the age of 9. How cool is that?

True story. "So, we are sitting at my Son's AB soccer practice. He's 7 at the time. The Sports complex is loud and chaotic from the gymnastic practices, Swim lessons, martial arts classes and the soccer practice. Now I knew Naomi was super quiet. I'm listening to lessons with my ear buds on and watching Abrams practice and something said turn to check on Naomi and I did. This is what my baby girl had drawn on her paper. It blew my mind that the whole time she was staring at me and she captured my essence in this drawing. Love her…
Parents nurture your children's gifts. They all have a purpose. You do to!

www.ingramcontent.com/pod-product-compliance
Lightning Source LLC
Chambersburg PA
CBHW040223220526
45473CB00001B/103